W9-CEX-364

Fact Finders®

Kids' Translations

Dr. Martin Luther King Jr.'s
I HAVE A DREAM SPEECH
in Translation
What It Really Means

by Leslie J. Holland

Consultant:
Dr. Clayborne Carson
Director, Martin Luther King, Jr., Research and Education Institute
Stanford University
Stanford, California

Capstone press®

Mankato, Minnesota

Fact Finders is published by Capstone Press,
151 Good Counsel Drive, P.O. Box 669, Mankato, Minnesota 56002.
www.capstonepub.com

Copyright © 2009 by Capstone Press, a Capstone imprint. All rights reserved.
No part of this publication may be reproduced in whole or in part, or stored in a retrieval system,
or transmitted in any form or by any means, electronic, mechanical, photocopying, recording, or
otherwise, without written permission of the publisher.
For information regarding permission, write to Capstone Press,
151 Good Counsel Drive, P.O. Box 669, Dept. R, Mankato, Minnesota 56002.
Printed in the United States of America in North Mankato, Minnesota.

052011
006155R

 Books published by Capstone Press are manufactured with paper
containing at least 10 percent post-consumer waste.

Library of Congress Cataloging-in-Publication Data
Holland, Leslie J.
 Dr. Martin Luther King Jr.'s I have a dream speech in translation : what it really means / by Leslie J. Holland.
 p. cm. — (Fact finders. Kids' translations)
 Summary: "Presents Dr. Martin Luther King Jr.'s speech and explains its meaning using everyday language. Describes the
events that led to the speech and its significance through history" — Provided by publisher.
 Includes bibliographical references and index.
 ISBN-13: 978-1-4296-2793-1 (hardcover)
 ISBN-10: 1-4296-2793-X (hardcover)
 ISBN-13: 978-1-4296-3449-6 (softcover pbk.)
 ISBN-10: 1-4296-3449-9 (softcover pbk.)
 1. King, Martin Luther, Jr., 1929–1968. I have a dream — Juvenile literature. 2. Speeches, addresses, etc., American —
Washington (D.C.) — Juvenile literature. 3. March on Washington for Jobs and Freedom, Washington, D.C., 1963 — Juvenile
literature. 4. African Americans — Civil rights — History — 20th century — Juvenile literature. 5. Civil rights movements —
United States — History — 20th century — Juvenile literature. I. Title. II. Series.
E185.97.K5H577 2009
323.092 — dc22   2008032867

Editorial Credits
Megan Schoeneberger, editor; Gene Bentdahl, designer and illustrator; Wanda Winch,
    photo researcher

Photo Credits
AP Images, 4, 8, 17, 20
Capstone Press/TJ Thoraldson Digital Photography, cover (bottom), 7 (top), 21 (left), 28
Corbis/Bettmann, 15 (both), 19 (right); Flip Schulke, 26 (bottom); Steve Schapiro, 26 (top)
Getty Images Inc./Hulton Archive/Shel Hershorn, 19 (left); Popperfoto, 13; Time Life Pictures/Don
    Cravens, 11; Time Life Pictures/Howard Sochurek, cover (Dr. Martin Luther King Jr.)
Library of Congress, Performing Arts Library, Sheet Music, 21 (right); Prints & Photographs Division, 7
    (bottom right), 23; Prints & Photographs Division, FSA/OWI Collection, 24; Prints & Photographs
    Division, NYWT&S Collection, 5, 25
National Archives and Records Administration (NARA), Charters of Freedom, 9 (left); Emancipation
    Proclamation, January 1, 1863, Presidential Proclamations, 1791–1991, Record Group 11; General
    Records of the U.S. Government, 7 (bottom left); Signed Copy of the Constitution of the United
    States, Miscellaneous Papers of the Continental Congress, 1774–1789; Records of the Continental
    and Confederation Congresses and the Constitutional Convention, 9 (right)

Essential content terms are **bold** and are defined at the bottom of the page where they first appear.

Table of Contents

CHAPTER 1
The I Have a Dream Speech
WHAT IT IS

Thousands of people gathered for the March on Washington and to hear Dr. Martin Luther King Jr. give his speech.

On the morning of August 28, 1963, about 50 people gathered in Washington, D.C., for a march. They stood in the shadow of the Washington Monument. At first, it didn't look like a very big march. But in a few hours the crowd had grown to about 250,000 people. There were black people, white people, students, lawmakers, actors, and reporters. They began their march to the Lincoln Memorial.

African Americans were tired of being second-class citizens. They wanted change. They wanted freedom and fair treatment. They demanded the same **civil rights** granted to white citizens. Many were angry enough to **riot**, destroy property, and hurt others. But not Dr. Martin Luther King Jr.

Dr. King used his words to inspire change. He used his actions to inspire peace. That was his dream. In 1963, he shared that dream with the world at the Lincoln Memorial in Washington, D.C.

Dr. Martin Luther King Jr.

civil rights — the rights that all people have to freedom

riot — to protest with violence

So what exactly does the speech say, and what does it mean to you? Turn the page to find out.

CHAPTER 2

The I Have a Dream Speech

WHAT IT MEANS

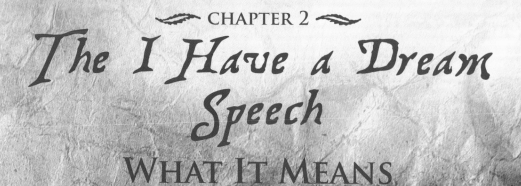

I Have a Dream Speech

Five score years ago, a great American, in whose symbolic shadow we stand today, signed the Emancipation Proclamation. This momentous decree came as a great beacon light of hope to millions of Negro slaves who had been seared in the flames of withering injustice. It came as a joyous daybreak to end the long night of their captivity.

But one hundred years later, the Negro still is not free. One hundred years later, the life of the Negro is still sadly crippled by the manacles of **segregation** and the chains of **discrimination**. One hundred years later, the Negro lives on a lonely island of poverty in the midst of a vast ocean of material prosperity. One hundred years later, the Negro is still languished in the corners of American society and finds himself an exile in his own land. And so we've come here today to dramatize a shameful condition.

segregation — the act of keeping one group of people apart from another

discrimination — treating people unfairly because of differences like race or color

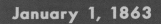

What?

One hundred years ago, President Abraham Lincoln signed the **Emancipation Proclamation**. It offered hope for slaves during the Civil War. They could see the end of slavery and the beginning of freedom.

But today in 1963, black people are still not free. The iron chains of slavery are gone. But they have been replaced by the chains of segregation and discrimination. Black people in America live on an island. All around them is wealth and plenty. But alone on their island, black people are poor and ignored.

In this document, Lincoln announced that all slaves in the Confederate states were free. But southern slaves still had to wait for real freedom. Slavery lasted until the 13th Amendment became law on December 18, 1865. It ended slavery in all parts of the United States.

7

I Have a Dream Speech Continued

In a sense we've come to our nation's capital to cash a check. When the architects of our republic wrote the magnificent words of the Constitution and the Declaration of Independence, they were signing a promissory note to which every American was to fall heir. This note was a promise that all men, yes, black men as well as white men, would be guaranteed the "unalienable Rights" of "Life, Liberty, and the **Pursuit** of Happiness." It is obvious today that America has defaulted on this promissory note, insofar as her citizens of color are concerned. Instead of honoring this sacred obligation, America has given the Negro people a bad check, a check which has come back marked "insufficient funds."

Whites protested against allowing black students to attend their schools.

pursuit — the act of trying to find or catch something

What?

The men who wrote the **Constitution** and the **Declaration of Independence** promised every American a check. It was to be cashed for freedom. But blacks have not been able to cash their check. Instead, they have been given a **bad check**.

On July 4, 1776, the 13 colonies announced their separation from Great Britain in the Declaration of Independence. In this famous document, Thomas Jefferson wrote that "all men are created equal." It also says that all people have certain rights, including "life, liberty, and the pursuit of happiness."

The U.S. Constitution became law on September 17, 1787. In 1791, the Bill of Rights was added to the Constitution. These rights include freedom of speech and religion.

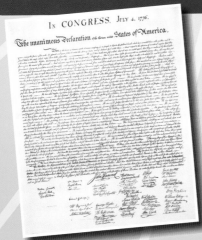

King didn't mean that blacks were owed actual money. He used the image of a bad check to stand for broken promises.

I Have a Dream Speech Continued

But we refuse to believe that the bank of justice is bankrupt. We refuse to believe that there are insufficient funds in the great vaults of opportunity of this nation. And so, we've come to cash this check, a check that will give us upon demand the riches of freedom and the security of justice.

We have also come to this hallowed spot to remind America of the fierce urgency of Now. This is no time to engage in the luxury of cooling off or to take the tranquilizing drug of gradualism. Now is the time to make real the promises of democracy. Now is the time to rise from the dark and desolate valley of segregation to the sunlit path of racial justice. Now is the time to lift our nation from the quicksands of racial injustice to the solid rock of brotherhood. Now is the time to make justice a reality for all of God's children.

It would be fatal for the nation to overlook the urgency of the moment. This sweltering summer of the Negro's legitimate discontent will not pass until there is an invigorating autumn of freedom and equality. Nineteen sixty-three is not an end, but a beginning. And those who hope that the Negro needed to blow off steam and will now be content will have a rude awakening if the nation returns to business as usual. And there will be neither rest nor tranquility in America until the Negro is granted his citizenship rights. The whirlwinds of revolt will continue to shake the foundations of our nation until the bright day of justice emerges.

What?

But we do not believe America has run out of justice. We believe America has huge amounts of opportunity in its vault.

We are here to cash the check that promises justice for all. The time is now. We will no longer wait. **Black Americans will not cool off.** We will not sit quietly, patiently waiting for our rights. Nobody will rest until blacks enjoy the rights promised to all Americans.

Black people had been protesting, demonstrating, and marching for almost 10 years. They were angry about their lack of rights in America.

The bus boycott in Montgomery, Alabama, began in 1955. Blacks refused to ride city buses for more than a year, until city officials were forced to end bus segregation.

I Have a Dream Speech Continued

But there is something that I must say to my people, who stand on the warm threshold which leads into the palace of justice: In the process of gaining our rightful place, we must not be guilty of wrongful deeds. Let us not seek to satisfy our thirst for freedom by drinking from the cup of bitterness and hatred. We must forever conduct our struggle on the high plane of dignity and discipline. We must not allow our creative protest to degenerate into physical violence. Again and again, we must rise to the majestic heights of meeting physical force with soul force.

The marvelous new militancy which has engulfed the Negro community must not lead us to a distrust of all white people, for many of our white brothers, as evidenced by their presence here today, have come to realize that their destiny is tied up with our destiny. And they have come to realize that their freedom is inextricably bound to our freedom.

We cannot walk alone.

And as we walk, we must make the pledge that we shall always march ahead.

We cannot turn back.

What?

But we must not break the law to get justice. We must not take away another's rights in order to get our own.

We must act fairly and **without violence**. When we are struck, we must not strike back. We cannot make white people our enemies. White Americans share the same fate as black Americans. We are in this together. We must move forward. We will not turn back.

King was inspired by Mohandas Gandhi. This leader used nonviolent protests to help India win independence from Great Britain in 1947. Like King, Gandhi believed in standing firm but never fighting back with violence.

Mohandas Gandhi

I Have a Dream Speech Continued

There are those who are asking the devotees of civil rights, "When will you be satisfied?" We can never be satisfied, as long as the Negro is the victim of the unspeakable horrors of police brutality. We can never be satisfied, as long as our bodies, heavy with the fatigue of travel, cannot gain lodging in the motels of the highways and the hotels of the cities. We cannot be satisfied as long as the Negro's basic mobility is from a smaller ghetto to a larger one. We can never be satisfied as long as our children are stripped of their selfhood and robbed of their dignity by a sign stating "For Whites Only." We cannot be satisfied as long as a Negro in Mississippi cannot vote and a Negro in New York believes he has nothing for which to vote. No, no, we are not satisfied, and we will not be satisfied until "justice rolls down like waters and righteousness like a mighty stream."

I am not unmindful that some of you have come here out of great trials and tribulations. And some of you have come fresh from narrow jail cells. Some of you have come from areas where your quest — quest for freedom left you battered by the storms of persecution and staggered by the winds of police brutality. You have been the veterans of creative suffering. Continue to work with the faith that unearned suffering is redemptive. Go back to Mississippi, go back to Alabama, go back to South Carolina, go back to Georgia, go back to Louisiana, go back to the slums and ghettos of our northern cities, knowing that somehow this situation can and will be changed.

What?

Some Americans think that the end of slavery should have satisfied us. But we cannot be satisfied. Not when the police beat us with clubs or **spray us** with fire hoses. Not when signs saying "Whites Only" keep us from motels, hotels, and other businesses. Not when black people cannot vote or have nothing worth their vote.

I know some of you here today have suffered. Some of you **have been jailed**. You have cuts and bruises from the way you were treated. But don't give up.

Police in Birmingham, Alabama, used high-pressure fire hoses on peaceful black protesters.

Even King himself was arrested many times for protesting.

I Have a Dream Speech Continued

Let us not wallow in the valley of despair, I say to you today, my friends.

And so even though we face the difficulties of today and tomorrow, I still have a dream. It is a dream deeply rooted in the American dream.

I have a dream that one day this nation will rise up and live out the true meaning of its creed: "We hold these truths to be self-evident, that all men are created equal."

I have a dream that one day on the red hills of Georgia, the sons of former slaves and the sons of former slave owners will be able to sit down together at the table of brotherhood.

I have a dream that one day even the state of Mississippi, a state sweltering with the heat of injustice, sweltering with the heat of **oppression**, will be transformed into an oasis of freedom and justice.

oppression — the treatment of people in a cruel, unjust, and hard way

Do not lose hope. We face problems today. We will face problems tomorrow. Still, I have a dream. My dream grew out of the **American dream**.

I have a dream that one day we will know what "all men are created equal" truly means. I have a dream that one day blacks and whites will sit down together at a table like brothers. I have a dream that one day **the state of Mississippi** will be a place of freedom and justice for everyone.

The state of Mississippi saw much violence during the civil rights movement. In 1962, University of Mississippi students rioted. They didn't want James Meredith, a black student, to start classes there.

The American dream is a term that means the idea of a happy and successful life.

White guards protected James Meredith on his way to classes.

I Have a Dream Speech Continued

I have a dream that my four little children will one day live in a nation where they will not be judged by the color of their skin but by the content of their character.

I have a dream today!

I have a dream that one day, down in Alabama, with its vicious **racists**, with its governor having his lips dripping with the words of "interposition" and "nullification" — one day right there in Alabama little black boys and black girls will be able to join hands with little white boys and white girls as sisters and brothers.

I have a dream today!

I have a dream that one day every valley shall be exalted, every hill and mountain shall be made low, the rough places will be made plain, and the crooked places will be made straight; "and the glory of the Lord shall be revealed and all flesh shall see it together."

This is our hope, and this is the faith that I go back to the South with.

racist — a person who treats people unfairly based on race

Today I have a dream that **my children** will be judged for who they are and not for their skin color. I have a dream that one day white children and black children will join hands. They will play together even in Alabama, although the **leader of that state** today is a man filled with racism.

I have a dream that all the hardships of today will soon be gone. We will all live together peacefully. This is the hope we share. This is the faith we take with us as we return home.

King and his wife Coretta Scott King had four children. Their daughters are Yolanda (far left) and Bernice. Their sons are Dexter and Martin Luther III (far right).

In 1963, George Wallace was Alabama's governor. He promised white people of the state, "segregation today, segregation tomorrow, segregation forever."

19

I Have a Dream Speech Continued

With this faith, we will be able to hew out of the mountain of despair a stone of hope. With this faith, we will be able to transform the jangling discords of our nation into a beautiful symphony of brotherhood. With this faith, we will be able to work together, to pray together, to struggle together, to go to jail together, to stand up for freedom together, knowing that we will be free one day.

And this will be the day — this will be the day when all of God's children will be able to sing with a new meaning, "My country, 'tis of thee, sweet land of liberty, of thee I sing. Land where my fathers died, land of the Pilgrims' pride, from every mountainside, let freedom ring!"

King lent his support to marches and protests throughout the south.

Because of our faith, we can have hope instead of hopelessness. With our faith, life will one day be peaceful. With our faith, we can go on with our lives knowing that real freedom is coming.

And we'll sing together when that day of freedom comes. And the words to an old familiar song will have new meaning. **"My country 'tis of thee, sweet land of liberty . . . "**

The words to the song *America* were written by Samuel F. Smith in the 1800s. Many people know the song by its first line, "My country, 'tis of thee."

I Have a Dream Speech Continued

And if America is to be a great nation, this must become true.

And so let freedom ring from the prodigious hilltops of New Hampshire.

Let freedom ring from the mighty mountains of New York.

Let freedom ring from the heightening Alleghenies of Pennsylvania.

Let freedom ring from the snowcapped Rockies of Colorado.

Let freedom ring from the curvaceous slopes of California.

But not only that: let freedom ring from Stone Mountain of Georgia.

Let freedom ring from Lookout Mountain of Tennessee.

Let freedom ring from every hill and molehill of Mississippi.

From every mountainside, let freedom ring.

And when this happens, when we allow freedom ring, when we let it ring from every village and every hamlet, from every state and every city, we will be able to speed up that day when all of God's children, black men and white men, Jews and Gentiles, Protestants and Catholics, will be able to join hands and sing in the words of the old Negro spiritual, "Free at last! Free at last! Thank God Almighty, we are free at last!

If America is to be a really great country, then freedom must be there for all. Let freedom ring from every state — north, south, east, and west. When freedom finally is allowed to ring, **all people** will be able to join hands. And in celebration we can sing, **"Free at last! Free at last! Thank God Almighty, we are free at last!"**

King hoped that all differences could one day be ignored. No matter what a person's religion, color, or other difference was, people could learn to get along.

A spiritual is a kind of religious folk song. The words to these songs were meant give slaves hope of freedom. The song *Free at Last* was published by John W. Work III. From 1946 to 1956, he published more than 50 spiritual songs.

CHAPTER 3

The I Have a Dream Speech

HOW IT CAME TO BE

Bus stations in the south had separate waiting rooms for blacks and whites.

In the United States, the new decade of 1960 was exciting and filled with possibilities. But for African Americans living in southern states, opportunities were few. Black citizens had a hard time finding decent jobs. They were kept out of the best schools. They couldn't buy a house or rent an apartment in the nicer areas of town. On public buses, they had to give up their seats to white passengers.

Many states in the south were segregated. Laws kept restaurants, movie theaters, drinking fountains, and public bathrooms separate. Black people could not enter places where a sign said "Whites Only."

In 1963, black leaders had an idea for a protest. They organized a march on Washington, D.C. Blacks would march for jobs and freedom.

One man was a natural choice to lead this march. Dr. Martin Luther King Jr. was a Baptist preacher and civil rights leader.

Bayard Rustin (left) and Cleveland Robinson helped organize the March on Washington for Jobs and Freedom.

King (holding megaphone) was a well-known speaker.

Born in 1929 in Atlanta, Georgia, King knew the sting of discrimination and worked for change. In 1955, he led black citizens in a boycott of the bus system in Montgomery, Alabama. He was known for his powerful, inspiring speeches.

On August 28, 1963, crowds gathered for the march and King's speech. Thousands of police officers were on hand to keep peace. But King's message was not one of hatred or violence. He spoke instead of his dream. His dream was that all people could live together in peace. His dream was that the United States would one day truly be the home of the free.

The words King spoke that day helped change attitudes in America. Before the end of the 1960s, laws were passed to give freedom to all of America's citizens.

King would not live to see his dream come true. He was killed in 1968.

Time Line

1929 — Dr. Martin Luther King Jr. is born.

1955 — Rosa Parks refuses to give up her seat on a bus to a white passenger. Her arrest inspires a bus boycott.

Nine black students are blocked from entering the all-white Central High School in Little Rock, Arkansas. Federal soldiers and National Guard troops are brought in to help the "Little Rock Nine" attend classes.

1957

1960 — At age 6, Ruby Bridges is the first African American child to attend an all-white public school in New Orleans, Louisiana.

1963 — The March on Washington takes place in Washington, D.C. About 250,000 people gather at the Lincoln Memorial to hear Dr. Martin Luther King Jr. speak.

1964 — President Lyndon Johnson signs the Civil Rights Act. The law gives the federal government the right to end segregation.

1965 — The Voting Rights Act is passed. It becomes easier for southern black citizens to register to vote.

1967 — The Supreme Court strikes down laws banning marriage between blacks and whites.

1968 — Dr. Martin Luther King Jr. is assassinated.

Why Do I Care?

5. On the third Monday in January, Americans celebrate the man who gave the I Have a Dream speech. Today the Martin Luther King Jr. holiday is observed in all 50 states.

4. King made another speech on April 3, 1968. In a Memphis, Tennessee, church, he called freedom the promised land. He said, "I may not get there with you. But I want you to know . . . we, as a people will get to the promised land." The next day he was killed by an assassin's bullet.

3. About 250,000 people marched to the Lincoln Memorial in Washington, D.C., to hear King speak in 1963. That's close to the number of people living in the city of Birmingham, Alabama, today.

2. King's words changed the course of history. Less than a year later, the 1964 Civil Rights Act was signed. Discrimination based on race became illegal.

1. The I Have a Dream speech was not just a speech about equal rights for African Americans. It encouraged tolerance and cooperation for all people no matter their race, religion, age, or other differences.

architects of our republic – No builders involved. These are the people who first set up the U.S. government.

bad check – A check is bad when there is not enough money in a person's account. The bank will return the check and not pay the amount written on the check.

dream — This kind of dream doesn't happen while you're sleeping. It's an idea of something that is perfect.

five score — The final score in a soccer game? No, a score equals 20, so five score is 100.

interposition — This may sound like a fancy job title, but it's not. It means stopping the federal government from enforcing federal laws.

nullification — This isn't a rotten vacation. It is the failure of a state to enforce federal laws.

soul force — It sounds like a disco group from the 1970s. But King was talking about a group of people acting together due to their spiritual beliefs.

Glossary

civil rights (SI-vil RYTS) — the rights that all people have to freedom and equal treatment under the law

discrimination (dis-kri-muh-NAY-shuhn) — treating people unfairly because of their race, country of birth, or gender

ghetto (GET-oh) — a poor neighborhood in a city where people of the same race live

inspire (in-SPIRE) — to influence and encourage someone to do something

oppression (o-PRESH-uhn) — the treatment of people in a cruel, unjust, and hard way

police brutality (puh-LEESS BROO-tal-uh-tee) — the act of a police officer using more force than necessary

promissory note (PRAH-muh-sor-ee NOHT) — a document signed by a borrower promising to repay a loan under agreed-upon terms

pursuit (pur-SOOT) — the act of trying to obtain something

racist (RAY-sist) — someone who treats people unfairly or cruelly because of their race

riot (RYE-uht) — to act in a violent and often uncontrollable way

segregation (seg-ruh-GAY-shuhn) — the practice of keeping groups of people apart, especially based on race

Internet Sites

FactHound offers a safe, fun way to find educator-approved Internet sites related to this book.

Here's what you do:

1. Visit *www.facthound.com*
2. Choose your grade level.
3. Begin your search.

This book's ID number is 9781429627931.

FactHound will fetch the best sites for you!

Read More

Dunn, Joeming W. *Martin Luther King, Jr.* Bio-graphics. Edina, Minn.: Magic Wagon, 2009.

Hinton, KaaVonia. *Martin Luther King, Jr.* A Robbie Reader. What's So Great About . . . ? Hockessin, Del.: Mitchell Lane Publishers, 2009.

Price, Sean. *When Will I Get In?* American History through Primary Sources. Chicago: Raintree, 2007.

Rappaport, Doreen. *Martin's Big Words: The Life of Dr. Martin Luther King, Jr.* New York: Hyperion Paperbacks for Children, 2007.

Index